Ashwell

SNIPPET
ASHWELL'S

Volume I

David Short

illustrated by
Phil Collins

Forewaord by
Lionel Munby

Ashwell Education Services

First printed 1997

Published by Ashwell Education Services
Merchant Taylors' Centre
Ashwell
Baldock
Hertfordshire SG7 5LY

Printed by The Print Works
Limlow
Litlington
Royston
Hertfordshire SG8 0RS

ISBN: 0 9529828 0 3

Contents

Foreword

by Lionel Munby

David Short came to work and live in Ashwell in 1975. During the twenty-one years since then he has immersed himself in the history of Ashwell, its human history, its architectural history and its landscape history. From the Merchant Taylors' Centre he has taught local history to school children, teachers and adult students. The result is that Ashwell has become a familiar and fascinating place to people throughout Hertfordshire and beyond.

In 1992 David began to share his knowledge with those who live in Ashwell by publishing a column in the monthly magazine, *Ashwell News*. Now he has put us all in his debt by bringing together many of these articles in a single publication which he has, modestly, called *Snippets of Ashwell's History*. From this we can, for the first time, really appreciate the width and depth of the knowledge of Ashwell history which David has acquired. Ashwell people are fortunate to have such an expert living amongst them and one who not only wants to share his knowledge but who can present it in an attractively readable form. David would not forgive me if I did not add that he, like all competent local historians, has learnt much from other local people whose research he has encouraged.

Lionel M Munby
October 1996

Introduction

In the summer of 1992 I decided to start a column in *Ashwell News*, the monthly village magazine edited by the Rector. I hoped that I might find enough material to keep me going for a couple of years, but was not sure what would happen after that. In the event *Snippets of Ashwell History* has been published every month since then and there is little sign of an end. The reason for carrying on for so long is partly because the material is there but also because people have not only encouraged me to keep writing, but have sent comments on particular topics, which I have then published. Other people have asked me to write on specific topics which, on the whole, I have managed to do. So my thanks go to all those who have made comments or suggested ideas.

I have been asked on a number of occasions if the *Snippets* were going to be published. This book is the result of those requests. The thirty-two *Snippets* in the collection were first published between September 1992 and December 1995. In this book the *Snippets* have been collected in topics and bear no relation to when they appeared in *Ashwell News*. I hope this will make the book sit together better.

I am grateful to Phil Collins for agreeing to illustrate this collection and to Lionel Munby for writing the Foreword. The illustrations are composites based on sketches drawn by Charlotte Morice in the 1840s, old photographs and the present day. They are not to be seen as illustrating a particular time. One other person has played a large part in the writing of the monthly *Snippets* and that is Eileen ten Hove. Her command of English grammar is far superior to mine and each month she tactfully and kindly corrects the errors of my ways. Many thanks to her. Eileen and Janice Murton also typed many of the *Snippets*, which I appreciate. Also Val high who read the manuscript and offered suggestions. I hope they enjoyed reading them at the time.

Any errors are mine and I would like to know about them so that they can be acknowledged and corrected.

I hope you enjoy reading this collection of *Snippets of Ashwell's History*.

David Short
November 1996

The History of Ashwell - in a Snippet

The village of Ashwell probably came into existence some time early in the tenth century. People have lived here since the Stone Age leaving behind them artefacts and evidence in the landscape. Ashwell Village Museum has objects from all periods from the Stone Age to the present day.

It is in the Bronze Age that we first find evidence in the landscape. Aerial photographs show many Bronze Age burial barrows besides the one called Highley Hill,[1] the only one which has not been ploughed out. Arbury Banks, a hill fort covering over 12 acres, was probably started in the Bronze Age before becoming the major site of the Iron Age in Ashwell. Once the Romans had settled in Britain in the first century AD fortifications like Arbury Banks were not needed and the site was abandoned. It appears that what is now the parish of Ashwell became a farming community based on the Roman town where Baldock is today. One such farm seems to be based on the building in what is now Pricems Field.[2]

Little is known about the history of the area between the Roman period and the later Anglo-Saxon period. That people lived here is evident from graves that have been excavated and from place names.

The creation of present-day Ashwell was probably in the early tenth century.[3] By 1086, when Domesday Book was compiled, it was the most important settlement, being a borough, a market town, in the area. The market place would have dominated the town and brought the wealth that is reflected in the number of quality medieval buildings, including St Mary's Church, that still exist today.

It would seem that the status of Ashwell did not last for long. Documents suggest that the sort of people one would expect in a

---

1 See *Highley Hill* on page 60
2 See *Pricems Field and a Roman Villa* on page 62
3 See *The Creation of Ashwell and Domesday Book* on page 48

thriving market town did not live here by the end of the thirteenth century.

By that time many other market towns had come into existence in the area,[4] and would have taken trade from Ashwell, which was not ideally placed, not being on any main roads. This does not mean that Ashwell had become a backwater. The building of the greater part of St Mary's Church during the fourteenth century points to the wealth of those who could afford to pay for it. It was during this building that the Black Death devastated England and left scratched on a wall of the tower the cry of those who survived this tragedy.

From 1350 to the early part of the nineteenth century it would seem that Ashwell stagnated. It was during this period that the flourishing market declined, so that by 1799 there was no longer an official market, although the last reference that can be found to a market existing is in 1862. It was during this period that Ashwell must have come to rely on agriculture as a source of income. Even so it was still near enough to London for those who could afford it to move into the country and yet be near enough to town when needed.

The nineteenth century saw some changes, with the growth of three industries, brewing,[5] coprolite digging and straw plaiting. As in most of England the population of the village grew during this period, reaching a high of 1,576 people in 1871, a size which was not overtaken until 1981 when 1,612 were recorded in the annual census. After 1871 the population held steady for two decades but declined between 1891 and 1901, when they stopped digging coprolites and the straw plait was not needed as much in Luton. In the twentieth century the two breweries closed - Pages in 1919 and Fordhams in 1966. In the latter part of the twentieth century changes in transport have brought a different life into the community. The motor car and rail travel mean that people can live in Ashwell but work elsewhere. These changes also bring traffic speeding through the village and parked cars fill the roads. But the village is a thriving, active community, where often it is difficult to find a night to hold a meeting or activity as there is likely to be something else already taking place.

4 See *Domesday Book and the Decline of Ashwell Market* on page 50
5 See *Fordhams Brewery* on page 22

People of Ashwell

Samuel Harradine

With all the emphasis today's newspapers have been putting on law and order it is probably just as well to remind ourselves that everything was not all that rosy in the past. The tale I quote this month also suggests an unusual place to spend a night!

At the Quarter Sessions on 27 May 1801 Samuel Harradine of Ashwell accused William Walker of Bygrave of beating him up. The Quarter Sessions were the meeting of the County Justices and were held four times a year. The origins of the Quarter Sessions go back to the middle ages as do most of the restrictions as to what cases they could hear. They were not allowed to hear civil cases but they could deal with murder, riot, theft, assault and poaching etc. In the published Session Rolls we read the following account:

Complaint of Samuel Harradine, of Ashwell. That on 23 May he was keeping sheep with William Walker, of Bygrave, in the fields of Bygrave, and deponent having put a wooden bottle in a hedge which William Walker afterwards could not find, the said William Walker threatened to kill the deponent if he did not find it. He threatened him again on Sunday and Monday, saying that if he did not bring the bottle that night he would 'properly dress him'. When deponent had that same night put the sheep in the fold, the said William Walker took him by the ears and beat his head violently against the earth and stopped his mouth full of earth to prevent his crying out. He then ordered him to fetch two fold sticks, one to knock the stakes in to fasten the hurdles and the other 'to leather him with'. He then so assaulted him that blood came from his ears and nose. Deponent then endeavoured to get home but could only go so far as the dunghill where he lay all night.

I wonder how comfortable a bed the dunghill made!

The Thorne Family

Those who have been into the Museum recently will no doubt remember the brass plate of 'S Thorne Builder' in the new gallery. This was Samuel Thorne, who is mentioned in the poem about the opening of the large classroom at the Centre. The last stanza starts:

> The school, all people must confess,
> A very handsome pile,
> Built by our Townsman, Samuel Thorne,
> Of ruddy brick and tile.

I found out a great deal about the Thorne family today from Heather Thorne, whose husband's grandfather lived in Pleasant Place in Hodwell, the house the family bought in 1724 and sold 240 years later. Abraham Thorne came to Ashwell in 1733 from Tempsford, having lived in Stansted before that. They were a Quaker family, although in 1807 Samuel was disowned by them for joining the militia and 'visiting a young woman not of our society in order for marriage ....'. It would seem that the Thornes followed three trades, wheelwrighting, tailoring and building. Pleasant Place was where the tailor lived and had his shop. I gather that the tailor's shop was in the older part of the house, the part to the left as you look at the front door. It seems likely that the brick part of the house was built by them. The wheelwright lived in the High Street where Wiles have their yard. This house and shop were burnt down in the fire of 1850. Another wheelwright lived in Ashe Cottage, which is next to the Merchant Taylors', or in a house between the two, which has since been demolished.

Many Thornes are buried in Ashwell. Those who were Quakers are buried in the Quaker Burial Ground, which is now surrounded by Angell's Meadow.

Samuel, the builder, born in Pleasant Place, having built the classroom, left Ashwell to become Head of Building Works for a firm in Vauxhall, London. It would be nice to think that the quality of his work in Ashwell secured him that job.

Robert Wilson

Albert Sheldrick and Norman Gurney's new book on Ashwell, *ASHWELL Village life in war and peace 1939-1975*, is fun to read mainly because it is about the people of Ashwell, people many of us know or knew. And so it is about history in general; it is usually the people who lived in the past, what they did and how they changed their environment that is of interest.

One character from the history of Ashwell is Robert Wilson. We do not know when he was born, but we do know something about his life. He first comes to notice during the period of the Commonwealth when, on 29 January 1646, the inhabitants of Ashwell petitioned the

Quarter Sessions in Hertford saying that he was 'a fellow of an unreformed wilfullness, to be a daily practiser of mischief, in cutting, spoiling, and carrying away men's grayne as it groweth in the fields. And the more to conceale his wicked practise hides it in his bed and elsewhere. And also one that will follow no lawful occupation but at excessive wages, who .... of his own authority to keep alehouse and therein to sell ale, daring us to our faces to do our best and worst, and with many an uncivil slighting and insufferable speeches, too tedious and unfit herein to relate, ... to the evil example of divers ill disposed people amongst us'. The next day John Sell complained to the Quarter Sessions that Robert Wilson had been heard to say that 'the cavaliers were coming to Ashwell, and if they did it should be his work to show them the houses of the Roundheads and where to plunder'.

What happened to Robert Wilson on that occasion I do not know. But ten years later it would appear that the inhabitants of Ashwell were still feuding with him. In that year he was indicted for 'erecting a cottage at Ashwell without laying four acres thereto'. This referred to an Elizabethan law which required anyone building a new house to have four acres of land, presumably considered sufficient to live on. This house still stands. It is the thatched house on the corner of West End and Wilsons Lane. The lane, formerly called Mill Lane, was renamed by the Parish Council in the early 1970s after Robert Wilson.

One of the odd things about Robert Wilson, presuming from the above that he had royalist leanings, is that in 1656 he applied for a pension from the maimed soldiers' fund. It seems likely that he got it as in 1661, with the new administration of Charles II, he was refused another pension. In the meantime he was up to his old tricks. In 1659 he was presented to the Quarter Sessions for stealing a bundle of barley from John Shipsea and in 1666 he was committed to gaol with others as 'dangerous and loose persons'. He was buried in Ashwell on 14 December 1687. By the way, his son carried on the family tradition when he was charged with assaulting Thomas Clarke, the constable, in 1668.

The Bryants and 19th Century Emigration

By 1832 the population of England was increasing rapidly, agriculture was in the doldrums, the Empire was growing - and the Government was trying to do something about it all. To help tackle these problems it was decided to encourage young agricultural workers to emigrate to the colonies. In February 1832 a booklet was sent to all parishes about 'Emigration respecting the British Colonies in North America'. The first line of the booklet tells us what it was about: 'The object of the present Notice is to afford such information as is likely to be useful to Persons who desire to Emigrate, or to assist others to Emigrate, to the British Possessions in North America'.

The sentiments of the booklet fell on fertile soil in Ashwell, as in 1836 the Parish assisted the passage of nine men between the ages of 18 and 28 to emigrate to Upper Canada, a part of Canada west of Toronto, north of Lake Erie. The Museum is fortunate in having some of the documents relating to the ticket for the 327 ton HARTLEY 'the fast-sailing NEW Ship'. The men were received on board on 25 May 1836 and given berths 35 and 36. It cost the Parish £5 per man for the trip from London to Quebec. The Colonial Office recommended that the Parish give each man sufficient money to make his way from Quebec to his final destination, but did not say how much.

We do not have any documents to say what happened to any of those men. However, the list included cousins James and Samuel Briant. Although we have no record of what happened to either man we do know that James's nephews emigrated there - Benjamin in 1854, Arthur in 1862 and David at an unknown date. Their father followed them between 1871 and 1880 after the death of his wife, Mariah. From this it would seem that there was correspondence between the families, with those in America encouraging those in Ashwell to follow them. The descendants of Arthur, the son of William and Mariah, today live in California. Contact was renewed some fifteen years ago and the two branches of the family still keep in touch.

TO SAIL PUNCTUALLY ON THE 25th MAY, FOR

QUEBEC, Direct,

The fast-sailing NEW Ship

HARTLEY, A 1,

327 Tons per Register.

ANDREW TURNBULL, Commander.

Lying in the London Dock.

This Ship has great height between Decks, and offers superior Accommodation for Passengers.

For Freight or Passage apply to the CAPTAIN, on Board; or to

CARTER & BONUS,
11, Leadenhall Street.

Abraham, Printer, 1, Clement's Lane, London.

The Fordhams and 19th Century Emigration

Responses to *Snippets* are always welcome and I am delighted to have received the following from Jeremy Fordham following last month's *Ashwell News.*

> I was very interested to read David Short's Snippets of Ashwell's History referring to emigration to the British Colonies in North America in the 1830s.
>
> Somewhat earlier than that, in 1817, ancestors of mine from Sandon and Ashwell emigrated with their Flower cousins to the American Colonies. In April 1816 George Flower, aboard

the ROBERT BURNS, set sail for New York, having been given a farewell party attended by seventy-three Fordham uncles and cousins. In 1817 he was joined in Cincinnati by Elias Pym Fordham and his family and they finally settled in Illinois. Elias Pym Fordham was an engineer having been apprenticed to George Stephenson who built the Rocket and it is said his engineering skills were invaluable. Elias Pym Fordham did not take to Illinois and later returned to England and was reported attending a Unitarian meeting at his father's house at Gannock in Sandon "chewing tobacco and talking American slang".

The Fordhams and their Flower cousins were both brewers in Ashwell and Stratford respectively. Also descending from the Ashwell Brewery was Ruddle's brewery in Oakham, Nora Fordham of Odsey marrying George Ruddle.

Other Fordham cousins emigrated to New Zealand in the 1850s and, two or three years ago, two of their descendants turned up at Odsey and my wife and I spent a happy afternoon showing them around the family parishes of Ashwell, Sandon, Therfield and Kelshall.

Buildings of Ashwell

Fordham's Brewery

In Ashwell talking about the changes brought about by the industrial revolution seems unreal. There are no great iron works or slag heaps. And yet there was a thriving industry which in some ways dominated the village. Brewing beer had been a cottage industry, but the Fordhams and Pages changed that, building an industry that was to give a livelihood to many people.

Fordham's Brewery is the one that is remembered today. It was the larger of the two and lasted longer. The story goes that in 1836 one of the Fordhams acquired brewing equipment from the publican of the Swan Inn, now Swan House, took it down Mill Street, set it up and started brewing. There is no evidence that I know of to substantiate this story, but it seems reasonable. Certainly by 1841 the Fordhams were in business, as the Tithe Apportionment lists Edward as having a 'House, brewery, farm building and garden'. Business boomed when coprolites were mined in the area from the mid 1850s to the end of the century and the thirsty workers needed something to drink.

The Fordhams did not restrict themselves to Ashwell. By the late nineteenth century they had pubs as far away as London, Ipswich and Bedford. Indeed as one drives into Hitchin, on the right sort of day, it is still possible to see the name Fordham in very faint paint on the roof of the pub on the left in Nightingale Road.

After World War II Fordham's could not compete, and before too long the brewing ended and only Guinness was bottled. On 1 April 1966 the brewery closed for ever. But some of the remains are still there in Mill Street. And some people can still describe the taste of the beer!

The Lychgate

The AGM of the Friends of the Museum gave those who were there new insights into one of Ashwell's well-known features. After the business meeting there were talks about the function and structure of the lychgate, based on the quarter-sized model which Tony Francis has built for me to use with children on field courses. As the model can be broken down into some 86 component parts it is an ideal way for children to learn how timber-framed buildings were constructed.

During the evening Adrian Gibson, an expert on timber-framed buildings, described how crown post roofs were constructed. One of the things he pointed out was that the lychgate did not always look as it does today. Not only were there probably shingles, small wooden tiles, on the roof but the gable ends were infilled with wattle and daub. If you go and look closely at the lychgate (and many who were at the talk have been been there), look up into the roof where you will see the collars - horizontal pieces of wood linking the rafters. It is the one at the north end that is of interest as it has some round holes in it. Careful inspection shows that there are similar holes on the large horizontal beam below it. These are holes to take the wattle, basket work or bits of timber, which was then covered with daub, a mixture of clay, chalk, dung and straw, so filling the gap between the timbers. This would have filled in the gable end. There is also evidence to show that the other end was similarly filled in.

The question 'why?' was raised. The lychgate was the place where the coffin or bier stopped and the first part of the burial service said. Before the eighteenth century most people were not buried in coffins but simply wrapped in shrouds, so it could be that the gable ends were filled in so as to keep out the rain. However, it would also give space for a picture, probably of St Mary, the patron saint.

If you look at the main posts just above the gates, you will see small, carefully carved niches. Were these spaces for small statues? The icons and the statues would have looked over, and, it was hoped, protected the soul which was making its last, and probably most important, journey.

Incidentally Tony, pointed out that the lychgate is not symmetrical, the side next to Mill Street being some 12 inches longer than the other. Any suggestions as to why will be received with interest.

The Lock-up

In the Village programme on Anglia TV in May I was seen to lock up a group of children in the Lock-up and walk away apparently without a care in the world. A few people have asked me what happened to the children; others seem to want to enlist my services! I can assure readers that the children are no longer in the Lock-up and that this is not a service offered by Ashwell Education Services.

The Lock-up, one of four surviving in Hertfordshire, was built in 1800. A chapel on the north-east corner of the chancel of St Mary's Church was taken down in 1799. The blocks of Totternhoe chalk were not wasted, but used to build the Lock-up. Incidentally, evidence for the chapel can still be seen; in the chancel there are two doorways, and the blocked up one would have led into the chapel.

There is a piscine on the outside wall of the church which would have been inside the chapel and there is a slight rise in the turf where the foundations are. These were seen in a recent excavation when a new gas pipe was laid.

But back to the Lock-up. It was originally used by the village constable to lock up people making a nuisance of themselves. After spending the night in the Lock-up they were taken to the magistrate in Royston the following day. It seems to have served this purpose until early this century. There is a story that recalls how Amos Pammenter and friends started making a nuisance of themselves after having spent a good evening in one of the many pubs in the village. The constable was called and Amos was put in the Lock-up for the night. While there his friends felt he needed further refreshment which they fed to him through the grille with the aid of a straw. They then went home. Amos however did not sleep and, getting bored, dug a hole under the door, crawled through and went home to bed. The authorities then decided that the Lock-up was no longer suitable for the purpose for which it had been built. It was left empty for many years, although it now appears to be in use again - not for locking up children I hasten to add.

The Lock-up is an interesting part of Ashwell history but in need of some vital repairs to the roof. Fortunately the Parish Council have this in hand.

Mills in Ashwell

Because of the need for flour to make bread, the grinding of corn has, until recently, been an important feature of people's lives. In early days this would have been done by individuals within the family, who would have used querns for the purpose. The Museum has a number of fine examples of these.

Domesday Book gives us the first reference to mills in Ashwell, listing three. These would have been driven by water, as windmills were not introduced into England until the fourteenth century. One of these mills would most certainly have been in Mill Street where the mill is today. The name Mill Street, or *le Mulnestrat* as it was written, was

used as early as 1299 and indicates that the site must have been in use then. Of the other two, one was probably situated just north of the sewage works, where the River Cam and the stream which forms the boundary with Hinxworth meet, in a field which was called Mill Corner in 1841. Unfortunately all remains seem to have been removed long ago.

It is to these mills that the peasants would have been forced to send their corn by the lords of the manors. The lay subsidy of 1293, a tax return, lists six people with the surname Miller. As surnames such as Miller would have indicated the person's occupation we can surmise that in that year there were six millers in Ashwell. Earlier and later lay subsidies have fewer. Over the centuries few millers are mentioned in documents although in the latter part of the eighteenth century there are some 10 mentioned in the militia lists. These however may not have all been millers of water mills.

While writing these *Snippets* I realised that I had no idea when the mill in Mill Street stopped working. I have checked all the references I can but have not found anything to tell me. Perhaps you know something about the history of this building in the twentieth century and could let me know. We know that the mill in Mill Street was working in the nineteenth century and at some time the large water wheel was abandoned in favour of a turbine, which still lies in the front garden. The wheel in the Mill today was rescued from Fordham Brewery when it was demolished in the late 1960s, and was never part of the mill. The buildings on the site were changed in the early 1970s when all but the Mill House was rebuilt. The picture on page 78 of *A Different World: Ashwell before 1939* by Albert Sheldrick clearly shows part of the mill buildings now demolished. The shed straddling the river and butting onto the road was at one time the Scout hut. But it would be nice to have more on file.

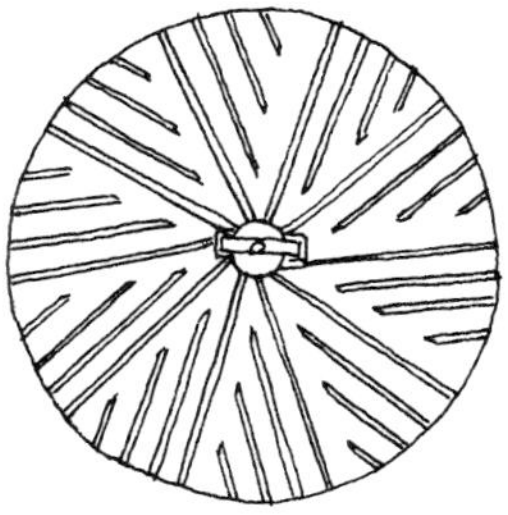

Merchant Taylors' School and the Museum

Researching the history of a house or building can be very frustrating. Many questions can be raised for which there are no immediate answers. For example, it might be interesting to know when an extension was built, the roof-line changed or a door relocated. All too often there are no written records as people have not kept the plans or accounts. Sometimes there are clues in the building itself which may give an indication, or there may be sketches or photographs. But the further back we go the more difficult it is.

Finding out about the people who lived in a particular house can be just as difficult, although sometimes researchers are lucky. There are two buildings in Ashwell that I have been interested in for some time

and with which I had some degree of success. My research into the Merchant Taylors' School House has revealed all the occupiers since it was built in 1681 except for the period 1713 to 1717. At that time the Revd Samuel Backler moved from the School into the Vicarage. It appears that he left the school empty, both of occupiers and boys. The villagers complained to the Company, who insisted he resign.

The other building of interest is the Museum. We are told that it was the Town House of the Abbott of Westminster. And yet in 1841 it was owned by St John's College, Cambridge. In a terrier, which is a list of property owned by an individual or organisation, of 1623 we read of *one Tenement situate betwene Clement Everitt on the west, And the Almas lane east.* This can only be the Museum and shows that St John's College owned it then. So far I have not been able to prove that the College owned it when it was built, probably around 1520, but I still hope to do so. I will let you know when I do.

Inventories and the Six Bells

In the last couple of weeks I have had the opportunity to look at the history of another house in the village. I wanted to mention the details of a probate inventory in a lecture I was giving in Cambridge and was looking around for a suitable one. I then remembered that the inventory of Richard Bygrave, who died in 1640, was just what I needed; it was the right period, the house it described had the right number of rooms and, most importantly, of the 85 inventories of Ashwell this is one of only two where I can be sure which house it refers to.

But, you ask, what is a probate inventory?

From 1529 to 1750, when a will was proved, the administrator was obliged to have an inventory of the personal estate (excluding land) of

the deceased drawn up and presented to the court. The appraisers listed the craft tools, farming implements, stock, corn, etc.

I know where Richard Bygrave lived and I know who his neighbour was. The 1609 deeds of the 'Angel' pub locate it firmly on the corner of Swan Street and Mill Street, in other words 'Swan House'. The deeds mention that the house of Richard Bygrave is on the east. This means Richard Bygrave lived on the corner of Swan Street and Church Path. The houses in between the two, including 'Miss Sim's House', were built more recently than 1609.

I then had a new problem - the rooms mentioned in the inventory, which included *a house called the shopp,* did not seem to relate to the present house, which suggested that the ground floor consisted of three rooms where there are now two. We know from a sketch of Church Lane done by Charlotte Morice in about 1840 that the house had a jetty - the first floor overhung the street - and would have looked like The Rose and Crown or Dixies Farmhouse do today. I then consulted a number of maps and found that the maps up to and including 1942 all suggest 3 rooms. The latest one I have, 1972, shows the present configuration.

What I would like to know is whether anyone can remember the house, which is called 'Six Bells' today, was 'Simply Scrumptious' in the late 1970s and the 'Six Bells' pub in the nineteenth century, being altered. It may have happened when Swan Street Garage, now demolished, was built. I think it probably happened in the 1920s but have no evidence. Or are the Ordnance Survey maps incorrect? I would like to hear from anyone who can shed any light on this problem.

More about the Six Bells

It is heartening to know that people read this column. Thanks to those who have stopped me in the street and commented. After the May issue, in which I wrote about the 'Six Bells' in Swan Street, I had a letter from Pearl Williams, nee Glasscock, of Stevenage, who lived in part of the building. She confirmed my thoughts that part of it had been pulled down this century.

Mrs Williams writes:

> As someone who grew up in Ashwell during the 30s and 40s, I can remember 'The Six Bells' as a pub, and I believe the landlord at the time was a Mr Frank Gentle.
>
> I enclose a photocopy of a snap taken in 1951, by which time it had been converted - probably for ten years or more - into two cottages, which each housed a young couple: the Harveys and Williams - my husband and I being the tenants of the one-up-one-down cottage ...
>
> We shared a tap across a cobbled yard with the other couple - also a toilet down the garden! Happy days!
>
> The owner of the cottage we lived in was a Mr Gordon of Cambridge, who offered it to us for £200 (two hundred pounds!) but it was beyond our means and we had never stepped inside a bank! So when we left Ashwell in 1951, a Mr Gallop bought the whole block and subsequently the other young couple were re-housed in Church Path where, sadly, a fire tragedy occurred a few years later.
>
> I would guess that the Swan Street Garage, built on the site of "our" cottage, was erected about the mid 50s.

Many thanks to Mrs Williams for this information and for permission to quote her letter.

PL HUDSONS
PAMPISFORD ALES

Church and Chapels of Ashwell

The Tower of St Mary's Church

The masons have finished their work and the west window of St Mary's Church can again be seen. Talking to the masons just before they finished, I was intrigued to find that they have used two kinds of stone to replace that which was damaged - Bath stone and Totternhoe stone. Both are limestone but have different characteristics. Bath stone has the distinctive yellow colour we associate with the city of Bath and is also hard and therefore durable. It has been used on those parts which are more likely to be vulnerable to weathering. Totternhoe stone is a local, softer stone which was used when the church was built in the fourteenth century.

Looking at the smooth, newly cut stone of the west window it is possible to imagine what the church must have looked like in the fourteenth century when all the stone was newly cut. Imagine what the people of medieval Ashwell must have seen when, on a late summer's afternoon, the setting sun changed the colour of the tower minute by minute. As most buildings in the village would have been lower than those of today the church would have appeared as an even more imposing structure and the effect of the sun on it even more dramatic.

Totternhoe stone, in its natural setting, can be seen at the springs. Under the gnarled roots of the large ash tree there are blocks of chalk. This is Totternhoe Stone. The chalk which we see in Ashwell starts here and then runs south under London and rises again in the South Downs. The chalk strata are made up of layers which were laid down over a period of some 30 million years. Depending on other factors individual layers may be hard, soft or somewhere in between. Totternhoe stone is a band of hard chalk which is good for building. Being harder than most chalk it lets less water through it and so it is that the water issuing from the springs comes from the cracks in the stone and not the stone itself. It is likely that the stone for St Mary's Church came from the quarry on the Hinxworth Road.

There is however one major drawback to using chalk as a building material. Being alkaline it reacts to acid. Most rain has a slight acid content and so there will always be some weathering. The

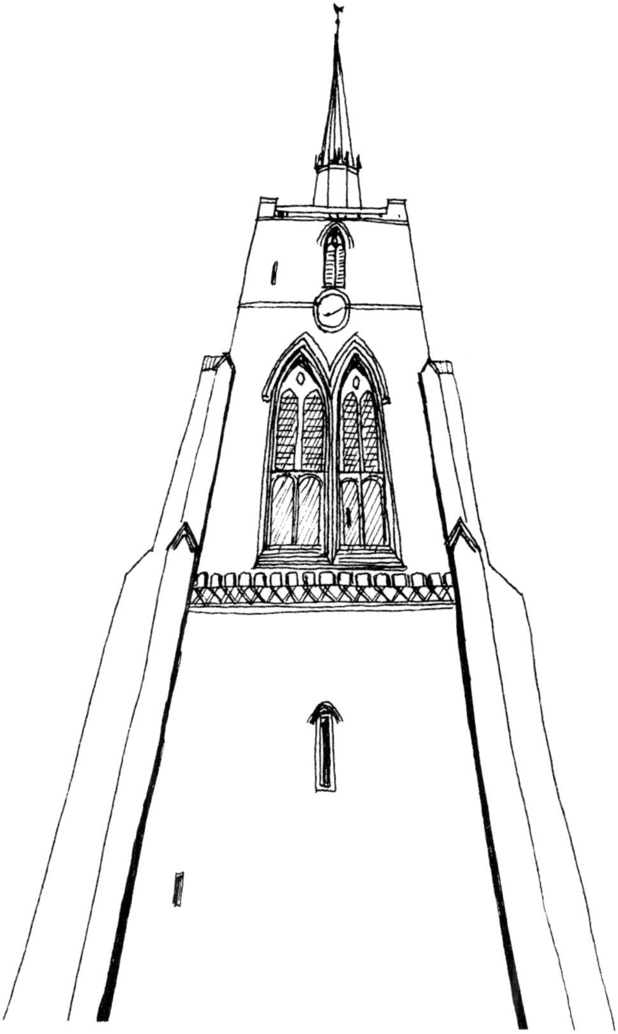

increase in acid rain this century has played havoc with buildings such as our church and we will continue to have large repair bills until such time as we find a way of reducing the acid levels in our rain.

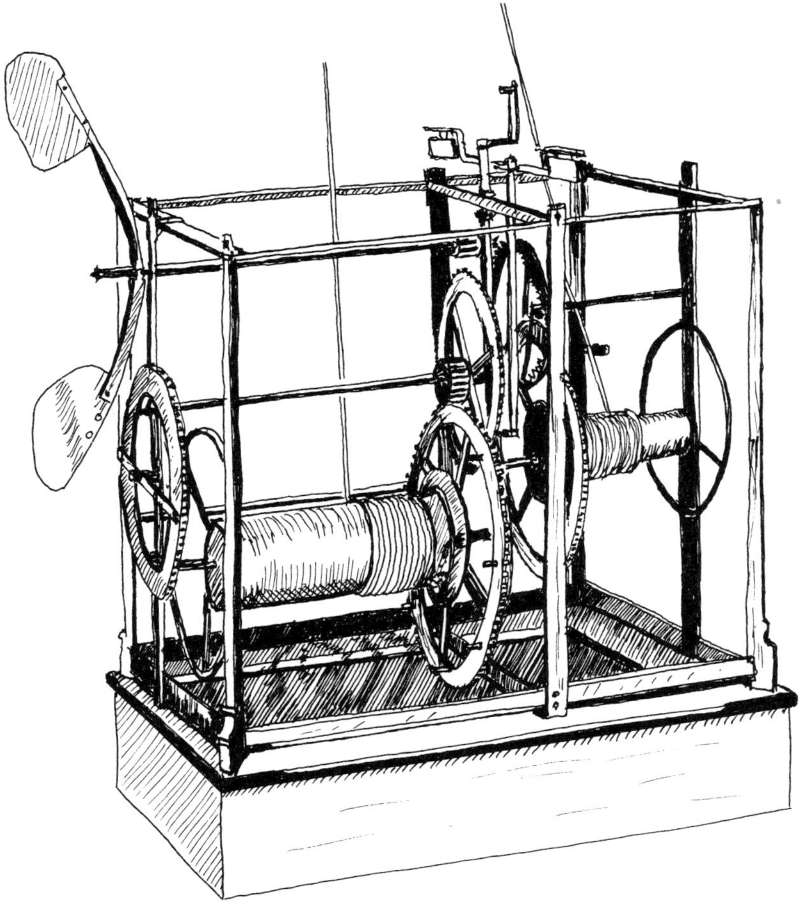

The 16th century Clock in St Mary's Church

As I have written before, accounts tell us a great deal about what concerned people in the past. Ashwell is fortunate in that many of the public accounts from the seventeenth to nineteenth centuries have survived, including those of the overseers of the poor, the surveyors of the highway, the constable and the churchwardens. Over the years some of these have been published so they are available for you to read.

My interest was roused when I first read the early churchwardens' accounts which have survived from 1562 - the state of some of the books is such that they are nearly impossible to read. In the Tudor churchwardens' accounts, which were published by the Hertfordshire

Record Society in 1985, we read of repairs to the church including paving for the church, lead and stones for the 'scholehouse', rope for the bells, 'bookes callyd the omelyes' and then '*Item* payd for a lock to the clokhowse'. The reference to a clockhouse raised my interest. There must have been a clock in the church in 1563/4. Two years later another entry states that 4d was paid for oil for the clock. Here then was evidence for the existence of a clock in the church long before the one on the wall in the south aisle or the one on the tower.

In most years between 1562 and 1602 money was spent on the clock, usually for oil or wire. Occasionally Thomas Cock of Newnham and others were brought in to mend it. In 1596 this included the use of nails and in the following year 'a styke a wood', whatever that was. In 1601 a further 4d was paid 'for 2 faggates to dress the clock'. The mind boggles as to what the 'faggates' were and what dressing a clock entails. Later in that year we read:

'it was concluded when the clock maker mended this owld clock being heer about yt 5 days that he should have for that and in consideration in bergayn for our new clock over and above fowerty shillings, five shillings to be payd presently'. So it appears that the clock mentioned as early as 1562 was no longer good enough and had to be replaced. Later in the year Thomas Arsnall was paid for a day and a half's work in setting up the clock and a new lock was put on the clockhouse door.

What can we say about the clock? I would think that some mechanism was placed in the church, possibly the tower, some time in the early sixteenth century. Unfortunately the records do not give details of the clock. However, there is a clock in Salisbury Cathedral which chimes the hours and quarter hours but does not have a face. This may have been a model for the one in Ashwell. It would have been heard over much of the parish, but there would have been nothing to look at. Perhaps one day other accounts will give an answer.

The Ecclesiastical Census of 1851

In last month's *Snippets'* I managed to get a date wrong! The Thornes bought Pleasant Place in 1824 and not 1724 as I wrote. They therefore owned the house for 140 years. Thanks to Heather Thorne for pointing out the errors of my ways!

In 1851, when the decennial census was done, an ecclesiastical census was carried out at the same time. Someone from each church and chapel, usually the clergy, had to give details of the establishment and the number of attendees on 30 March. The figures are interesting. The parish church was reported as having seating for 1,000 people. On 30 March it recorded 150 general congregation and 150 Sunday scholars in the afternoon. There was no evening service.

There are two returns for the Independent chapel; one in March and one in October. The Chapel was burnt down in the fire of February 1850 and the rebuilding was not completed until October 1851. Nevertheless, the Chapel reported seating for 280 and a general congregation of 252 and 65 Sunday scholars attending in the evening of 30 March!

The Wesleyan chapel, which was in Church Lane and built in 1833, had seating for 266 people. On 30 March there were 80 general congregation and 70 Sunday scholars in the morning; in the afternoon there were 276 and 71, and in the evening 250 general congregation. The Sunday scholars were let off in the evening! The last return was for the Mill Street Meeting of the Particular Baptists. They did not say how many they could seat, but 20 could stand. In the evening of 30 March 36 general congregation attended. It is difficult to say where this meeting was held. The manager of this chapel was Allen Flitton, the miller at Radwell, and it was not until the 1870s that his family built Little Garth as well as the Baptist Chapel in Gardiners Lane. In 1851 some of the Flittons lived at the Bury and, as the Fordhams, who owned the Bury, were Unitarians, I wonder if the meeting was held there.

Considering the total population of Ashwell in 1851 was 1258 it is interesting to speculate on the accuracy of these figures.

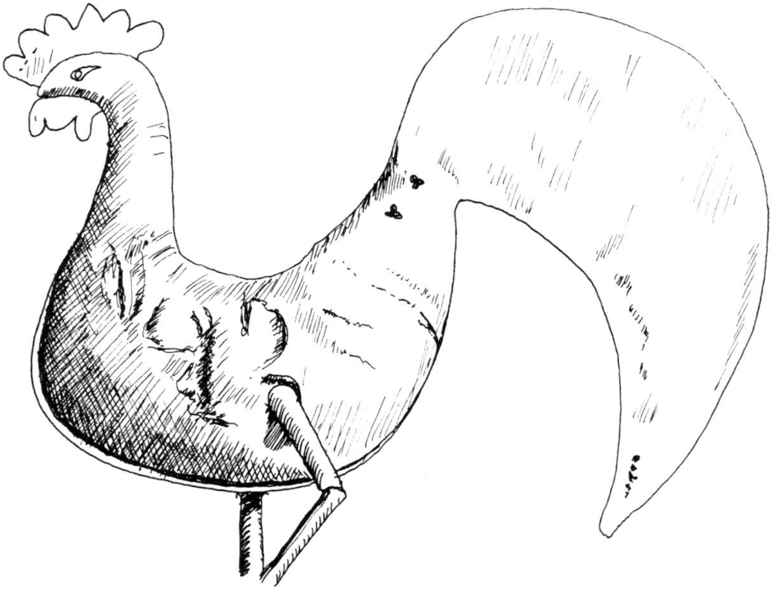

The Weathercock on St Mary's Tower

I was recently given a report from the *Herts & Cambs Reporter*, now the *Royston Crow*, of 3 December 1909 which I found of interest. An article, titled "The Weather Cock" was abut Ashwell. I quote:

> A considerable amount of interest has been taken in the thrilling and perilous work of the Steeple-jacks upon the steeple of the Parish Church. Mr. J. Royds and assistant, of the firm of Mr. T. J. Driscoll, of Birmingham, have overhauled the leads to the apex of the structure 175 feet from ground, removed the vane, refixed a new spindle and ornamental iron scroll work (made by Messrs J. W. Pack & Son). "The

> Bird", a fine piece of copper work, has been re-gilded by Mr. A. Hoye, and now surmounts the grand old edifice ready to face a thousand storms. This is the first renovation for the past 43 years. Upon the comb of the bird, stamped in copper, is the following, "W. Westrope, churchwarden, 1822". Upon a careful examination there are certain drilled holes which have presumably drilled out the original churchwarden's name and year. The first hole drilled out the initial for the Christian name and the four holes the surname; further the year 1822 proves that the first inscription has had [the] date changed. Mr. Royds, the practical expert in lightning conductors engaged upon the repairs, practically condemns the existing one, but the authorities appear to be satisfied that this is not a necessary work.

It would seem from this that the cock was placed on the steeple in 1822, renovated in 1866 and in 1909. There was a further renovation in 1947/8 after it had been blown off in a gale in 1947 - there is a picture of Fred Bray and Albert Sheldrick replacing it in *ASHWELL Village life in war and peace 1939-1975.* I gather that the time has come for it to be renovated yet again.

It would be interesting to know if the weather cock placed on the steeple in 1822 was the first one. Unfortunately the earliest drawings we have of the church are those by Charlotte Morice from the late 1830s, so this source does not help. I have looked through a few of the churchwardens' accounts but have not found any reference to it there. Perhaps someone else would like to try!

Miscellaneous

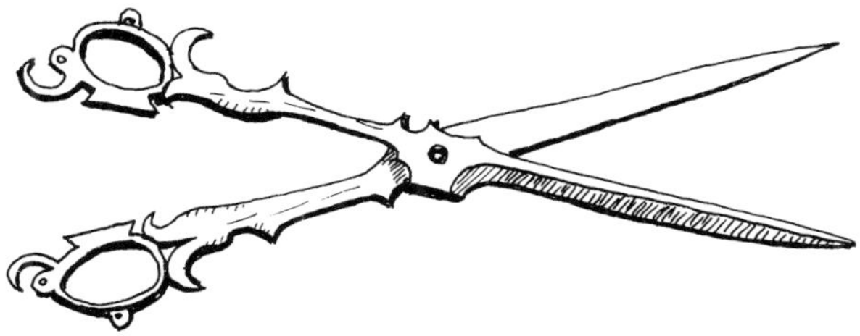

The Creation of Ashwell and Domesday Book

We do not know when the village, as opposed to the parish, of Ashwell was created. The layout of the roads and other circumstantial evidence suggest that it was a deliberate creation, probably late in the ninth century. The first reference we have to Ashwell is in the will of Aethelgifu who lived in Tempsford, Bedfordshire. She left 20 sheep to Ashwell. What happened to the sheep we do not know. What the document shows us is that Ashwell, as a parish, existed.

The next reference we have is in 1065 when Edward the Confessor gave the manor and rectory of Ashwell to the Abbey of Westminster. As Ashwell is only one of many places mentioned in the charter we are not given details about the settlement. The first detailed reference is in Domesday Book of 1086. The four references to Ashwell suggest that there were two manors in the parish, the main one being the one held by Westminster Abbey and probably referring to the village itself. There are 87 people mentioned in the four entries. As the people are not mentioned by name but by status the 87 probably represent the heads of households. This would make a population of between 450 and 600. Of the 87 one was a

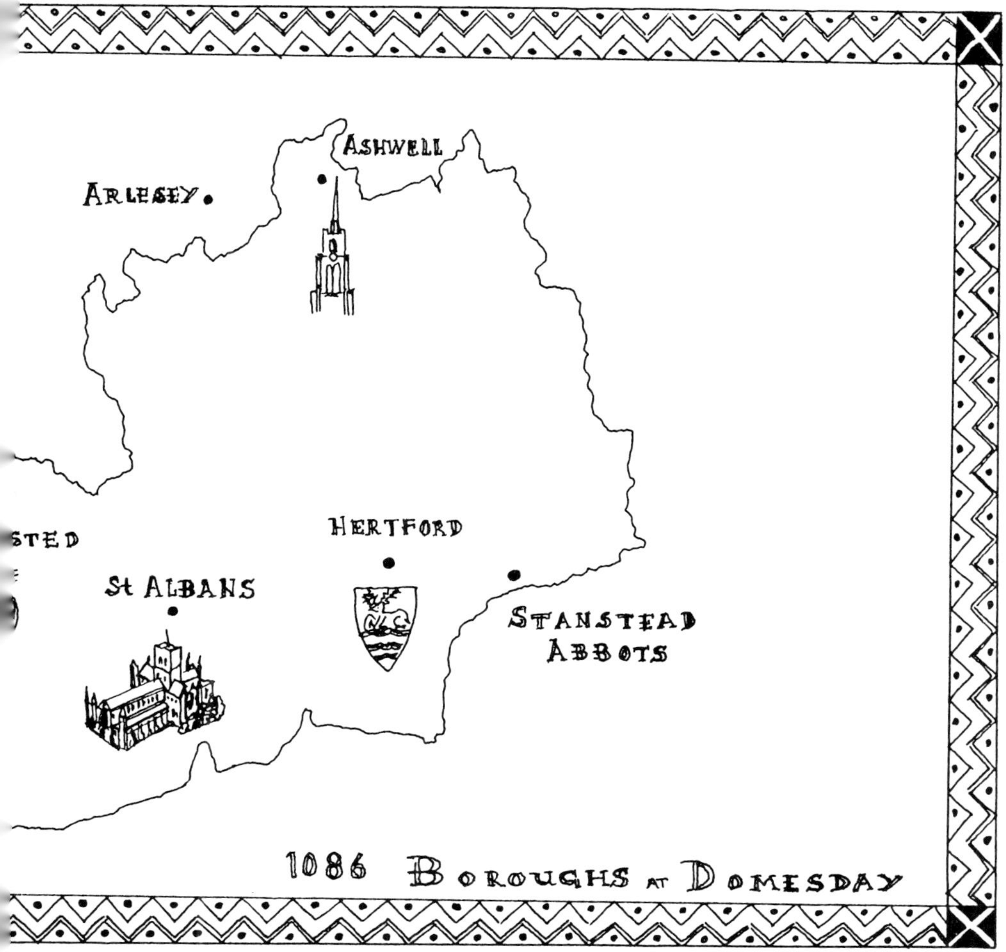

priest and there were 14 burgesses. The reference to burgesses, who had rights over the market place, and the reference to Ashwell being a borough, tell us that Ashwell was a market town, one of five in Hertfordshire. In terms of population size we know that Ashwell was larger than Stanstead Abbots, slightly smaller than St Albans and smaller than Hertford and Berkhamsted. Ashwell was, however, the most important town in this area. Looking beyond Hertfordshire the closest boroughs were Cambridge and Bedford. Even today the Ordnance Survey maps show roads entering Ashwell from all directions, testifying to its importance in the past.

Domesday Book and the Decline of Ashwell Market

For some time I have thought that it would be interesting to do a regular column in the *Ashwell News* on aspects of the history of the village. Research often yields up little quirks that give us insights into how the people of Ashwell lived in the past. No doubt members of the Ashwell Local History Group, which meets on a Tuesday evening from September to April, will add pieces. Maybe some other readers would like to send their memories or stories about the past to me.

I am fascinated by the fact that at the time of Domesday Book Ashwell was a thriving borough, a market town, and yet today it is a village, albeit a thriving one. What caused the change in the status to Ashwell and when did it occur? Two bits of evidence may help to shed light on the problem. Surviving in the Public Record Office in London are many tax returns, some, the lay subsidies, going back to the thirteenth century. These lists of tax payers were drawn up at a time when surnames were starting to be generally used, and so the surnames are an indication of where people have come from, their nickname or their occupation. In the lay subsidies of 1291, 1293 and 1307, the earliest ones to survive for Ashwell, there is no indication that Ashwell is still a borough - a bustling market town yes, but not a borough. So it could be that by this date Ashwell had already lost its status.

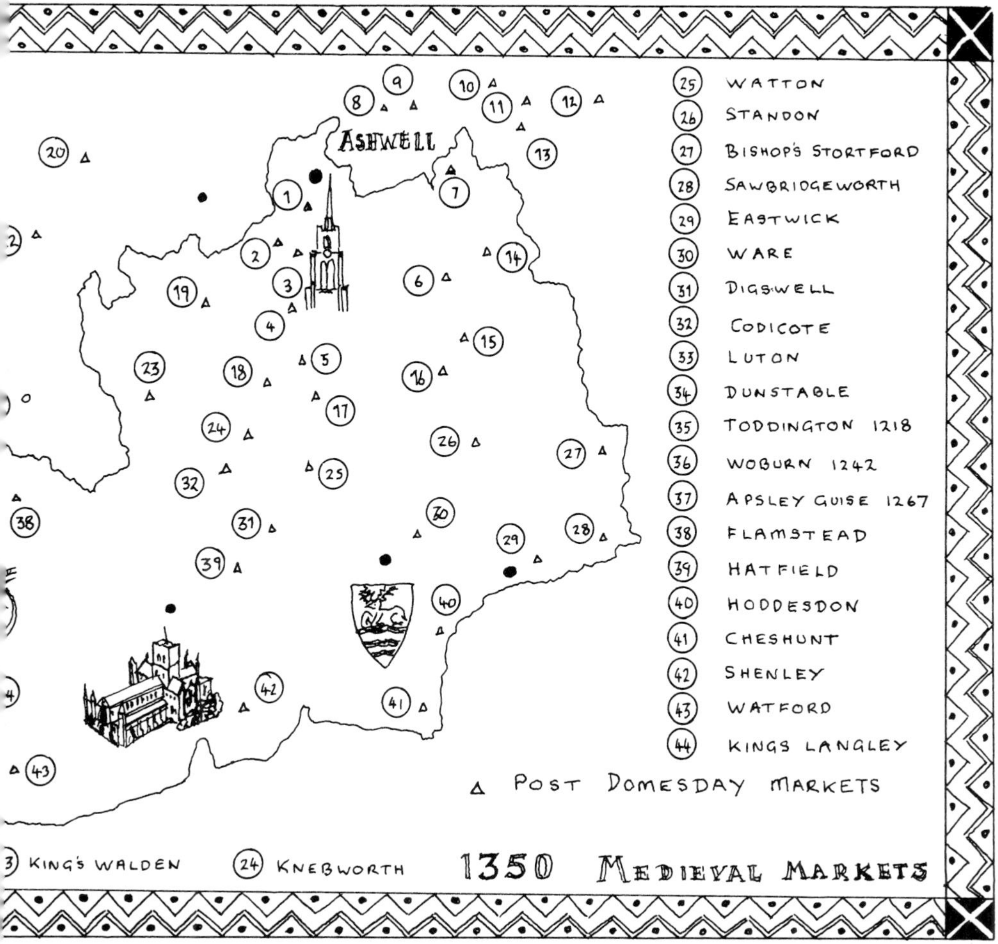

But why? Domesday Book shows very few market towns in the area. Arlesey was one, but very small. Other than that, one had to go to Bedford, Cambridge, Saffron Walden, Hertford, Stanstead Abbots or St Albans. This means that in 1086 Ashwell was by far the most important town for miles around. By 1300 the pattern was very different. There were markets at Bassingbourn, Royston, Baldock, Hitchin, Stevenage, and many more places. In other words by 1300 people could do their shopping in places other than Ashwell, and like those who in recent years used to shop in Letchworth, they went somewhere more convenient.

Changes to New Year's Day

Now that Christmas and New Year are over there is an opportunity to reflect on the fact that the celebrations we have just had were not always the norm in England. Before 1750 Christmas Day would have been a much more muted affair, not dissimilar to many other days of the year, and there would have been no celebration on 31 December and 1 January to bring in the New Year.

The reason for the lack of festivities was that New Year's Day was not 1 January. Until 1752 New Year's Day was on Lady Day, that is 25 March. This meant that December was the tenth month, not the twelfth. However, it does not explain why our tax year begins on 6 April. That is something I will return to on a future occasion.

What has this to do with Ashwell? Most people know that the graffiti in the tower of the Church is about the Black Death of 1350. Below it, also in Latin, is a reference to a storm 'that thundered in the world' on St Maur's Day in 1361. As St Maur's Day is on 15 January in our calendar, it happened in 1362 and not in 1361. This presents a problem to authors - if writing about the storm in which year do they say it happened?

The storm that the graffiti refers to affected not only the lives of the people in Ashwell. It appears to have been a storm similar to those which hit the south-east of England a few years ago when trees were blown down and houses damaged. The storm of 1361/2 damaged the tower of Blackfriars in London and the tower of Norwich Cathedral. Little wonder then that the people of Ashwell, whose houses were built of timber placed directly on the ground without any foundations, would have been frightened and would have sought refuge in the church tower, where the 7 foot thick walls would have offered some sort of protection.

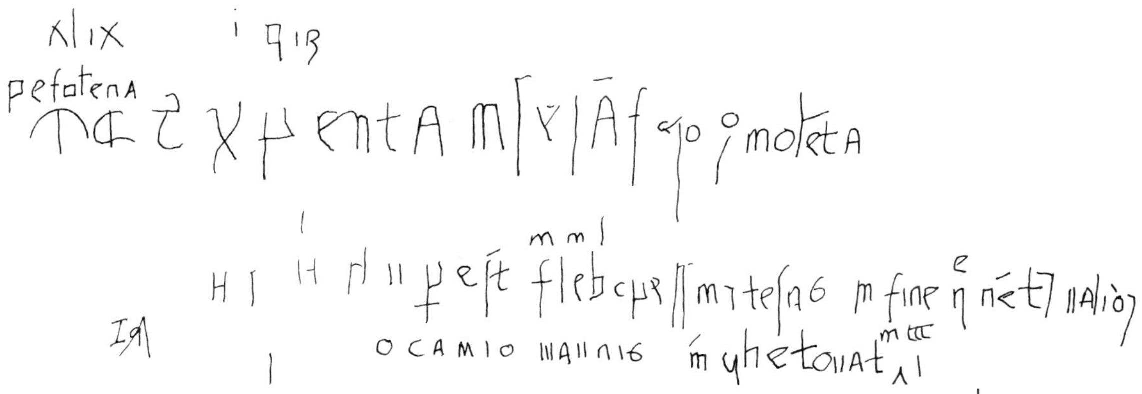

John Betjeman on Ashwell

Being nosy helps when you are a local historian! A couple of weeks ago I was taking a stroll around the village in the evening when I saw some people videoing the horses in Church Mead. Knowing that an ITV crew was coming to Ashwell I went to have a chat. They had nothing to do with ITV, who have been making a programme to be seen in January, but were making a video on John Betjeman. I was curious as I was not aware that John Betjeman had written anything abut Ashwell. It transpired that for many years he had written a column in the *Spectator* and in July 1956 had written about Ashwell. Of the village he wrote:

> So I went to Ashwell which is near nowhere, unless it be Baldock, and on the road to nothing, thank God. ..... We first saw its gigantic dark grey fourteenth-century church tower, crowned with a tapering lead flèche, rising from huge elms on chalky foothills looking over open corn land to the levels of Hunts and Cambs. The main street to the village wound with varying vistas

> of colour-washed cottages, white and orange and pink, half-timbered and grey-green local nineteenth-century brick. And here and there were gaps of orchard between the houses and views through veil beyond veil of elm tree rows of further pastoral quiet. There were lanes lined by thatched walls leading to the wooden mill and puritan chapels and to a big house built by Lutyens. ... on one corner we saw the best cottage garden I have ever seen, without even a path except for cobbles that led to the cottage, and across its roses and poppies we saw an old umber-washed corner house and above it, dominating all, this magnificent church tower. And the church inside, white and spacious and East Anglian, with arcades like a cathedral, clear glass everywhere, uneven floors and splendid chancel, was worthy of the best of English villages.

Which makes me wonder what else there is that has been written that I, and others like Peter Greener, Curator of the Museum, are not aware of. Someone recently asked me about a book on the history of Ashwell written in the 1940s. I have never heard of it. If you know of any unusual mentions of Ashwell please let me know. We need to have copies in the village.

Roads of the Parish

Discovering the past of any place often leads down some strange paths. In March members of the Ashwell Local History Group and friends were taken on a walk to see the evidence for ancient roads.

For some years Mike Buzzard has been researching the roads of the parish, where they were and their changing names. Evidence comes mainly from maps and documents as well as from the landscape itself. The maps and documents tell only part of the story, with the landscape offering tantalising clues about the parts not covered.

The first stop on the walk was the gateway to Westbury in the West End. The question Mike posed was 'why does the road have the S bend and not go straight?' The tithe map of 1841 and the enclosure map of 1863 help in that they show a footpath from West End to the Hinxworth Road. So far no documents have been found that give further details, but Mike is confident that the landscape offers clues. The bumps and other manmade features show that at some stage the road did not bend but carried on along the high ground to the south of the drive to Westbury, across the field to Hinxworth Road and then across the next field to Caldecot Way.

The walk took us along Caldecot Way, which prior to enclosure in 1863 was one of the principal routes out of Ashwell. We saw evidence, albeit a very slight bump in the path, for an ancient road called Poulters Way which by-passed Ashwell. On reaching the parish boundary with Newnham we walked down to Newnham Way. On the way we were able to see the remains of the strips ploughed out at enclosure. We walked across Newnham Way and up the footpath past the piggery, where we saw further evidence of roads no longer used.

The walk was fun. Some felt that being asked to believe that small bumps in the ground were evidence of roads which had possibly disappeared centuries ago was asking too much. But it did make us look harder at the landscape around us. Mike is planning another walk in a different part of the parish in the late summer. If you are interested please contact him or the Centre. More details of the Local History Group are also available from the Centre.

Christian Names in 1851

Since 1801 a national census has been taken every decade, except for 1941 when a world war took precedence. It was in the eighteenth century that the Government realised that it needed details of the population in order to plan ahead. The first censuses were just counts of heads. In 1841 personal details were taken for the first time. Because of the sensitivity of the material the personal details are not released by the Public Record Office for 100 years.

So it was on 1 January 1992 that the detailed Census Enumerators for 1891 were released. I recently had the opportunity to start analysing these when I was asked to do some work on nineteenth century Ashwell with Class 1 of Ashwell JMI School.

We analysed Christian names in part of the village. We found that the three most popular girls' names were Mary with 34, Elizabeth 27 and Ann 15. The three most popular boys' names were John and William, 27 and George, 22. These are not names that are common in Class 1 today. Other research I have done shows that these are the most popular Christian names in the period 1600 to 1881 in Ashwell.

Among the 74 girls' names we found similarities with today. Emma, Charlotte, Hannah, Rebecca and Sarah were fairly popular.

Among the 41 boys' names 18 are to be found in the Bible. They include Joseph, Benjamin, Levi and Matthew. There were also historical names - Arthur, Henry/Harry and Albert being the most popular.

We thought we might find a few of the girls called Victoria after the Queen, who had by then reigned for 64 years. There was only one. Maybe the memory of her husband was more popular - there were 6 Alberts, even though he had been dead for 40 years!

Many thanks to Class 1 for their help.

Highley Hill

The prehistoric times of Ashwell are not well researched and documented. However, this does not mean that we do not know anything about them.

There is one Bronze Age feature in the landscape that is easily seen. This is Highley Hill which, because it is on private land, has to be seen from a train. Leaving Ashwell Station the train passes Odsey House on the south and then runs alongside the park. The north side of the track has bits of woodland and cultivated fields. Once past the park a look on the north side reveals a small copse on the horizon with an earth mound to the east looking rather like a pimple. This is

Highley Hill, a grave built as the last resting place for someone from the Bronze Age. This barrow, as this mound is called, is not the only one that was made in Ashwell and the surrounding area. At the right time of the year the careful observer will see a slight rising in the middle of the field to the south of the railway line. This is the remains of a well ploughed barrow which is much better identified on aerial photographs. Between it and Highley Hill, again on the north side of the track, yet another one can be identified on aerial photographs.

The dry summers of 1975 and 1976 offered a good opportunity to fly over Ashwell in a light aircraft to look for signs of past features and changes to the landscape. During flights evidence of a number of barrows in the chalk hills to the south of the village were seen. Interestingly there were none on the flatter land to the north. Evidence is seen from the air in dry summers as the corn grows to different heights and at different rates on soil that has been disturbed. This means that just before harvest, in the right light, shadows are cast by the sun on the longer corn showing images of the past. As the corn ripens it does so at different rates, again showing the activity of people in the past. For about a week last summer the road which once went from the corner of Ashwell Street and Station Road to Slip End was clearly visible from the Guilden Morden road due to the different colours of the corn.

This suggests that there must have been people living in the area who could sustain a fair number of large graves. Whether they were only for the important people of the community or for all we do not know at present. But there may be more for us to find out in the future.

Pricems Field and a Roman Villa

Life in what is now the parish of Ashwell must have changed radically in the years after 43 AD, the year of the successful Roman invasion. Prior to the invasion Arbury Banks was the centre of life, offering a place of refuge, when necessary, for those who lived nearby. With the coming of the peace and stability of *Pax Romana* the need for a defensive hillfort disappeared and the people could live elsewhere.

Baldock became the local town and it seems likely that farms were created around the region. One such farm house, or villa as they are usually called, was discovered in Pricems field in 1970. Pricems is the field on the north side of the road going from Ashwell to Bluegates, between Buttway Cottages and Berefords. The stream that runs along

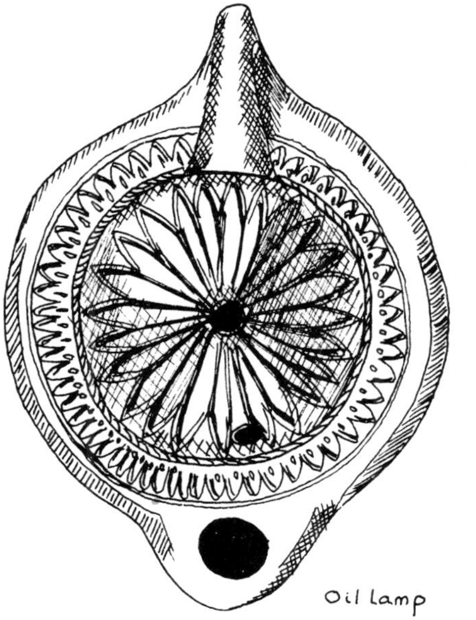

Oil Lamp

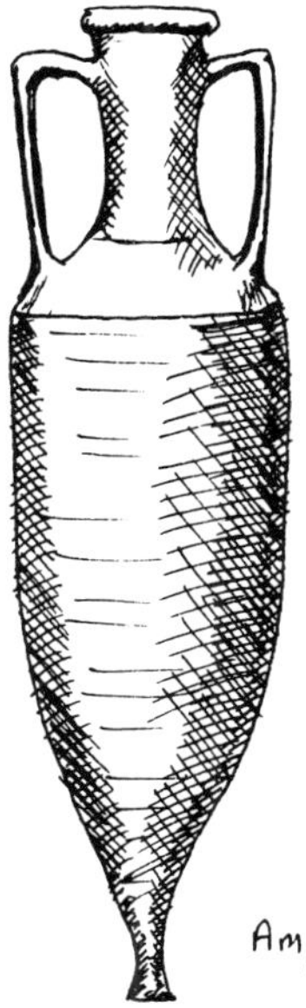

Amphora

and then under the road crosses Pricems, bisecting the villa site. In 1970 Pricems had been ploughed, probably for the first time ever, when John and Susan Morris, out for a walk, noticed that the field was littered with Roman materials. That afternoon, John, a Roman scholar, together with Richard Higham, an archaeologist, measured the site and collected and recorded the surface material. The results were interesting. The spread of materials, which included clunch, roof and flue tiles, fine quality and coarse pottery, and oyster shells, suggested a villa comprising buildings on three sides of a central courtyard and measuring some 70 yards by 80 yards. There was probably a bath house in the south-west corner. A proper excavation was never carried out so we do not know the exact size or the arrangement of the rooms. The finds from the site suggest an occupation period from the second half of the second century until the later fourth/early fifth centuries.

Today we would probably say that this was a substantial farm house. We have no idea of how big the farm was, or indeed where the fields were. Roman fields tended to be rectangular and it could be that the square marks in the fields just north of Bluegates and on either side of Bennetts Lane, which can be seen in aerial photographs and sometimes from the ground, indicate fields attached to the villa. But this is speculation on my part. Maybe you know better!

Governing Ashwell

The Overseers' Accounts and Poor Relief

From Anglo-Saxon times until Henry VIII dissolved the religious houses, monasteries took care of those in need of support - the homeless, the sick, etc. Henry VIII's changes led to problems in this respect and, during the later sixteenth century, there was a rising problem of 'vagabonds and rogues'. To counter this the Poor Law was enacted at the end of Elizabeth I's reign. Under the Poor Law parishes were responsible for those within the parish who fell on hard times. Each parish elected two overseers of the poor each year who for six months would distribute relief from their own pockets. At the end of the year they presented their accounts to the vestry meeting and, if approved, a rate was levied on the parish and they were reimbursed. These accounts were kept and those for Ashwell which survive start in 1677 and carry on into the nineteenth century.

The overseers' accounts record two aspects of relief. Firstly, weekly pensions. So we might find a widow receiving 1 shilling (5p) per week, or a family man 2s 6d (12½p) per week. Some of the entries seem to show two widows living together, probably in the alms

houses that were in Alms Lane, behind the Parish Room. Secondly, other disbursements were for incidental items such as helping a man who was ill or injured and could not keep his family; clothes for destitute women and children; burying the poor and keeping the workhouse.

The parish rented the workhouse, which in the eighteenth century appears to have moved from building to building. In the 1730s rent of £8 0s 0d a year was paid to Mrs Mary Carter. The fact that the area in front of the Museum is called Carters Pond, and the fact that the row of houses between Mill Street and Gardiners Lane was called Workhouse Yard in the 1841 Tithe Apportionment, suggest that this was the building.

The accounts also show the money spent on food and other necessities for the inmates of the workhouse. On 8 June 1728 the overseer John Carter, Mary's husband, bought 41¼ lbs cheese, 3 lbs butter, 2 lbs sugar, 8 dozen eggs, some plums, oatmeal, salt and 5 pecks of peas. This seems to have been the food for the week. Rent paid for the gravel pits and for spinning suggest the work that the men and women were doing and also how some income was generated. It appears that the master of the workhouse was being paid 1shilling (5p) a week for each inmate.

The Governing of Ashwell

The recent Parish Meeting and the Parish Council elections have made me reflect on what we know about past elections and the organisations which ran the village.

In medieval times each manor had a court which, like the House of Lords today, made laws as well as trying infringements. A parish could have more than one manor, which meant that different people in the parish would have allegiance to different courts. However, when it was necessary for all the people of the village to agree on aspects of common interest, all would meet as the *community of the vill*, a democratic assembly where the lord of the manor had an equal place with the peasants. This meeting would decide on matters such as when animals were to be put on to the open field, and when the gleaning was to take place - in other words, issues which were important to everyone.

The court immediately above the manor court was the hundred court. A hundred was an area comprising a group of parishes, not too dissimilar to the district council of today. Above the hundred court were the Quarter Sessions, the county justices meeting four times a year.

Over time things changed. By the sixteenth century the churchwardens had become a power within the parish, although strictly they were only responsible for the church. At the end of that century legislation was passed requiring the election of overseers of the poor in each parish. By the eighteenth century there was an annual meeting, called the vestry meeting, when the churchwardens, the overseers of the poor, the parish constable and the surveyor of the highways were elected. To manage this there was a vestry clerk who, more often than not, was the schoolmaster at the Merchant Taylors' School. Besides electing the officers for the following year the vestry had to agree the accounts of the officers and, on agreement, to levy the rate so that the officers, who had made payments from their own pockets, could be reimbursed.

Occasionally there where hiccups. In 1774 William Mann, the overseer of the poor and also the publican of the Rose and Crown, had his accounts rejected. The minutes record: 'It appear'd to the Vestry that several Frauds had been intended to have been imposed on the Parish, therefore the Vestry were of Oppinion that a Prosecution should be commenced against the said William Man. But he appearing in Vestry and Acknowledged that he was Innocent, that it was thro' the ignorance of his Wife and Son, and that he had not the least intention to Cheat or Defraud the Parish. He begged that the Vestry would compromise the Matter with Him.' This they did as they agreed not to prosecute if he repaid the outstanding £18 13s 1d.

Vicars and Rectors

Prior to 1867 Ashwell had a vicar. In that year Henry Hodgson became Rector of Ashwell. As the distinction between a parish with a rector and one with a vicar can be a bit confusing I thought I would attempt to throw some light on the subject.

Until 1223 Ashwell would have had a rector who was the incumbent who received all the tithes as well as customary offerings and dues. In 1223 Pope Honorius III gave possession of the church of Ashwell to the Abbot and Convent of Westminster. Eighteen years later the Bishop of Lincoln, in whose diocese the parish lay, constituted it a

vicarage. The vicar was a deputy appointed to care for the parish on behalf of an institutional rector. This means that Ashwell had both a rector (the Abbot) and a vicar (the incumbent), whose names are on the list in the church. When the Abbey of Westminster was dissolved by Henry VIII in 1540 a new Diocese of Westminster was created. The rectory of Ashwell, together with other rectories formerly held by the Abbey, was given to the new diocese. Eleven years later, when the diocese was dissolved, Ashwell was given to the Diocese of London. So from the mid-sixteenth century the Bishop of London was rector of Ashwell and appointed the vicar.

By the mid-nineteenth century further changes had taken place in the church and the position of the Rectory was reconsidered. As the Diocese of Lincoln went from the Humber to the Lea, and the population of the country was changing rapidly, part of the Diocese of Lincoln, including Ashwell, was taken away to form part of the Diocese of Rochester. But this did not suit the rapidly changing needs of the time and in 1877 the Diocese of St Albans was created to embrace Hertfordshire and Bedfordshire. Ashwell became part of yet another diocese.

The difference between a rector and a vicar involved the receipt of tithes. Tithes were a tax of one tenth of all the produce from the land and labour given to the church. Traditionally the larger tithe, the harvest of arable land, was given to the rector and the lesser tithe, that produced from stock and labour, was given to the vicar. These tithes constituted the income for the rector and vicar. Over the years tithes were converted to cash payments. In Ashwell from 1241 the Bishop of Lincoln confirmed that all the tithes, together with the house, were settled on the vicarage, the Abbot and Convent of Westminster receiving 38 marks annually and income from old barns, the farm, the market and the water-course belonging to the church mill. This made the vicarage of Ashwell one of the most wealthy livings in Hertfordshire.

In 1867, following a change to the law, Ashwell became a rectory, although not all the tithes paid were to be the income for the new rector. However, in 1870 the income was £513 per annum with the vicarage, a large sum for the times. In the 1920s and 1930s the position of tithes was reviewed and abolished. Thereafter the incumbent was paid a stipend.

'Ashwell Water for Ashwell People'

Continuing the theme of local government from last month it is interesting to reflect on the way piped water came to Ashwell in the early part of this century.

Traditionally people got water from the springs, the river or a well. In more recent times many had pumps. Sewerage was left in holes in the ground or in ditches. Following new ideas about sanitation in the nineteenth century cities started to install sewage systems and piped water. In London the piped water was not new, as wooden pipes were used in the seventeenth century to take water to Eastcheap.

During the nineteenth century concern about the sanitary conditions in Ashwell grew. In 1855, after an outbreak of smallpox, the surveyors of the highway were authorised to remedy the filth in parts of the village. By 1878, within the Royston Union, Ashwell was notorious as the most insanitary and diseased parish. In 1886 the medical officer found many wells were largely contaminated with sewage matter. In 1896 the Rural District Council wrote to the Parish Council 'respecting the unsatisfactory condition of a public ditch at the West End'. The reply from the Parish Council was that they 'thought the village of Ashwell was in a healthy state and the death rate very low [and] that they thought a system of sewage was not necessary'. But a case of typhoid in 1897 in Back Street made people realise that there was a need for a proper system.

The Parish Council decided that it would go ahead with a scheme to bring water into the village as well as removing the sewage. But the wheels of bureaucracy moved slowly. A decision had to be made as to where the water came from - was it to be piped from Toplers Hill near Biggleswade, or would a borehole be sunk in the parish? Decisions were made and then contradicted. Quotes were received, and advice from government departments and loans applied for. All of this took time and by 1910 there was still no action. In that year there was an election for two seats on the Rural District Council. Four men stood - Webb, Fordham, Bowman and Rogers. The first two supported the Toplers scheme, the other two the Ashwell scheme. The Ashwell supporters won. After further debate and changes of mind it was eventually decided to sink the borehole at the waterworks on Bygrave

Road. A windmill was used to pump up the water to be stored in the reservoir and then fed by gravity to the houses of Ashwell. At the same time a sewerage system, ending in the filter beds at Ashwell End, was installed. In September 1913 the work was completed and the final certificates signed.

There must be some lessons to be learnt from this!

TREMENDOUS EXCITEMENT.

VOTE! ! VOTE! ! !

FOR

BOWMAN & ROGERS

The Men who are fighting for the People's Rights.

Ashwell Water for Ashwell People

and the People's Rights will be Won. ! ! !

Printed and Published by J. Mason, Royston.

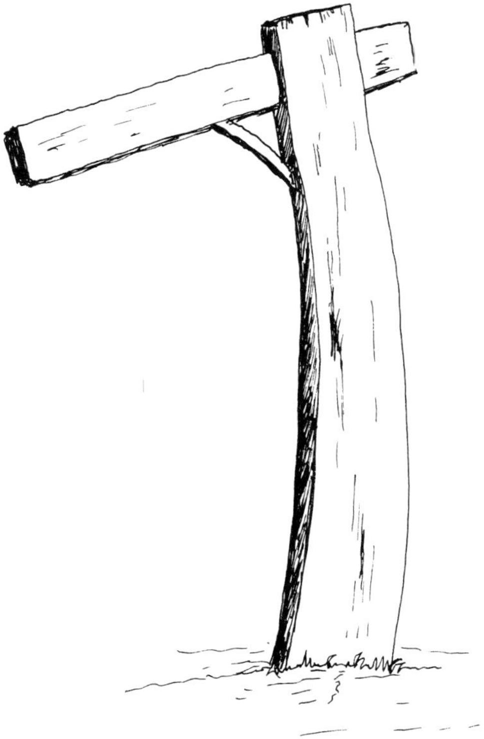

Justice during the Reign of Elizabeth I

The administration of justice has always been dealt with at various levels. Less serious crimes were, and still are, dealt with at the local level, whereas more serious crimes were dealt with by courts either in important towns, i.e. county towns, or in London. However, to bring justice to the people it has been a long tradition for some courts to travel around the country. For example, from the middle ages until the nineteenth century, serious crimes were dealt with by the Justices of the Assize. So it is possible, by searching the records of the assizes, which go back at least to the fourteenth century, to find out more about the worst crimes committed in Ashwell.

A few years ago calendars of the Hertfordshire Assizes for the reigns of Elizabeth I and James I were published. Although unfortunately they do not have all the detail of the original records, we do get a glimpse of what was going on at that time.

The first Ashwell case in these calendars is in May 1575 when Thomas Burforde, a dyer, and Edmund Burforde, a labourer, both of Baldock, were found guilty of stealing 48 sheep to the value of £12 from Edward Sawell of Ashwell. Stealing stock was a serious crime and four of the seven cases which were brought before the assizes to do with Ashwell in the reign of Elizabeth I were to do with stock theft. Besides this case there were two other cases of sheep theft, one 'not guilty' verdict being returned, and one case of cattle theft. The men who stole the cow ventured as far as Anstey to perpetrate their deed and still did not get away with it! Of the other cases one was for murder. On this occasion James Thompson was found guilty of strangling the widow Helen Thompson. Of the last two cases, the first is about two people who were accused of coining, i.e. making a 12-penny piece from base metal, and the second about John Seelie, a tailor from Hoddesdon, who was hanged for highway robbery having been found guilty of stealing 24 shillings from Thomas Dawson in the highway at Ashwell.

The reign of James I produced far more cases, but avid readers of *Snippets* will have to wait for a future *Ashwell News* to read more.

Merchant Taylors' School

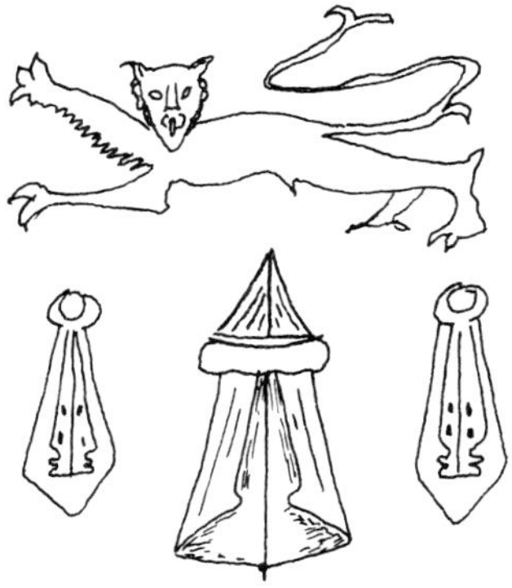

Henry Colbron, Founder of the Merchant Taylors' School in Ashwell

Over the last year much has been said about the future of the Ashwell Merchant Taylors' School. Perhaps now is the time to think about its history and, more particularly, its foundation.

Early in the seventeenth century Henry Colbron moved from Kirkham in Lancashire, where he was born, to London where he was apprenticed as a scrivener, a writer of legal documents. He obviously did well. When he finished his apprenticeship he gained the freedom of the Worshipful Company of Scriveners. In time he was to become a livery man, a member of the Court, and later a Warden. He lived in Walbrook in the City.

As was common at the time, men who had made money in the City bought property in the home counties. We do not know how he became connected with Ashwell but some time in the 1640s he bought the lordship of the Manor of Westbury in Ashwell. Later, during the Commonwealth, he also bought some of the land of the Manor of Ashwell.

On 1 August 1655 he made his will and seven days later died. In his will he bequeathed all his lands in Ashwell and elsewhere to his son, James. But as James was under 21 there were conditions. If James was to marry or die before he was 21 then the property was to be bequeathed to others. One of the beneficiaries was to be the Merchant Taylors' Company, who were to receive 'One Thousand pounds to purchas lands for the erecting of a Free Schoole & purchasing lands for the Endowment & maintenance therof to bee kept in Ashwell County of Hartford And I give the said Company One hundred pounds for their paines and also for the Nominacion of a Scholemaster there forever'. Fortunately for Ashwell, James died in 1662 when he was 20 years and ten months old and engaged to be married. Later that year the Merchant Taylors' Company, probably to their surprise, found that they had to build and maintain a school in Ashwell as well as finding and paying a schoolmaster.

It was in 1902 that they handed over the running of the school to Hertfordshire County Council. However, they continued, as they still do, to have an active interest in the activities of the School, whilst still administering the Henry Colbron Trust.

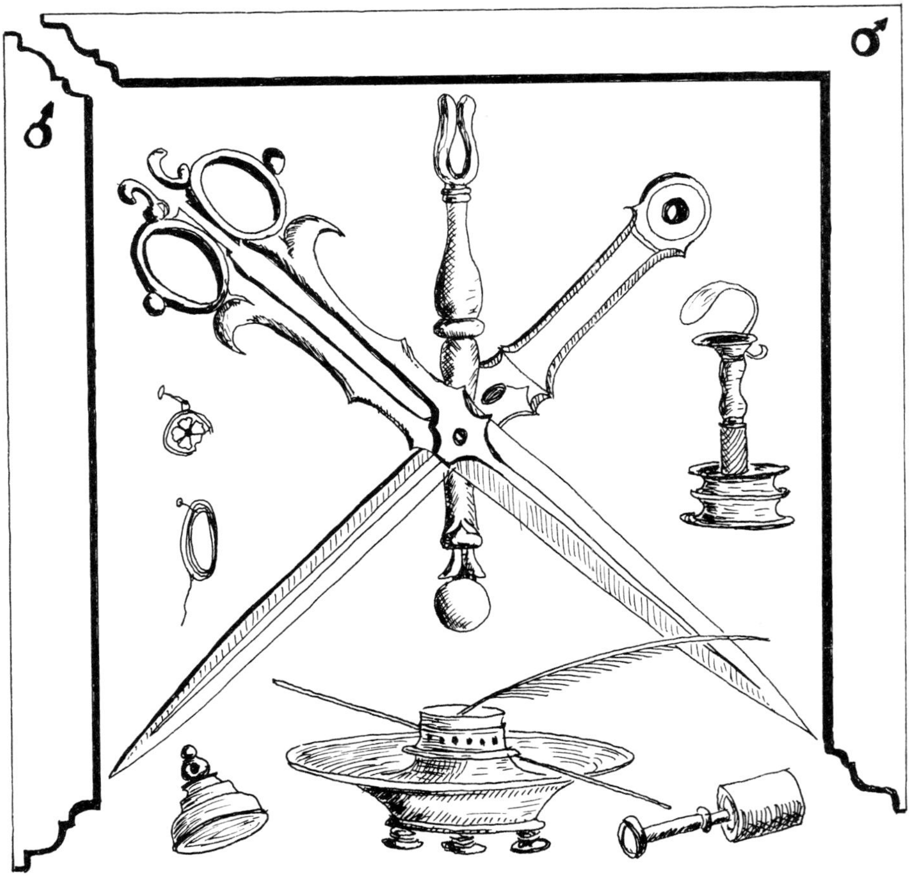

More about Henry Colbron

Recently I had the pleasure of meeting someone related to Henry Colbron, the man who bequeathed the money to the Merchant Taylors' Company to found the school in Ashwell. Having found out about the Centre, Mr and Mrs Colborn (the spelling has changed over time) came in to see if there was anyone who could tell them anything about Henry and the school. I spent a few happy hours talking to them. Mr Colborn's ancestor was the brother of Henry. Henry's son died aged 20 and unmarried.

From this meeting I was able to find out a bit more about Henry Colbron than I wrote in *Snippets*, August 1993. His family lived in Freckleton Street in the parish of Kirkham, Lancashire where they were tenants of a burgage, a burgage being a property, usually a house and yard, with a small street frontage and a long strip of land behind. There was further land attached to the Colbrons' burgage. After his father's death in 1623 his mother took on the lease of the property which he then acquired three years later. Henry appears to have had three sisters and two brothers. His brother later took on the tenancy after him.

For some reason unknown to us Henry decided in 1615, when 16 years old, to seek his fortune in London. In London he was apprenticed to his uncle James who was a Scrivener. We do not know why he moved to London, but it could be that it was felt that he could do better there and there were relatives besides Uncle James in the south-east. In 1624 Henry gained the freedom of the Company of Scriveners which meant that he could then practise within the City of London. In 1640 he became an Assistant of the Company (in effect a member of the board) and in 1653 a Warden, one of four men who assisted the Master.

On 10 February 1640 he married the widow Anne Bass at St Dunstan Stepney. They lived in Walbrook, the road alongside the Mansion House, but worshipped in the parish of St Antholin. This may suggest that his property backed onto the parish of St Antholin and so was near the corner of Walbrook and Budge Row. He was active in the parish, serving as churchwarden in the 1640s. He is also mentioned a few times in the church records. He died before his wife on 8 August 1655 and was buried the following day in the Church of St Giles Cripplegate, the church in the centre of the Barbican complex. Why he was buried there and not in his own parish I do not know, but he was obviously well thought of as his marble tomb, now sadly gone, had on it a poem which included the words:

> Silence! but a word, namely, that he
> Was pious, wise, just, merciful and free; ...
> Pardon his meaner grave, who thought it meet,
> By virtue, not with fabrics, to be great,
> For in this tomb none could more trophies bring.

Recent Changes to the Merchant Taylors' Centre

Over the last two years, 1992 to 1994, many people in Ashwell have been concerned about the future of Merchant Taylors' Centre. In April last year over 120 people squeezed into the classroom at the Centre to express their views to those concerned. At last the matter has been sorted out and it seems therefore appropriate to explain what has happened over the past three years and give a brief preview of the future.

Changes in education initiated in the late 1980s appeared to threaten the future existence of the Centre. Part of the problem was that, although the County Council runs the Centre, different departments within the authority had responsibility for different activities - the Library Service for the Library, the Education Department for the Field Studies, North Herts College, which at that time was part of the Education Service, for Further Education and for the site as a whole. But if one of the three was to withdraw would the other two be able to take on the added costs?

In November 1991 it was clear that my job, as Advisory Teacher with responsibility for the Field Studies Centre, was in jeopardy. It seemed likely that I would be moved to Wheathampstead and the Field Studies activity at the Centre brought to an end. I thought it highly unlikely that the Library Service and North Herts College would accept additional running costs; the entire Centre would then have closed. Therefore, in December 1991, I approached the County Council and offered to take redundancy and take over the running of the Centre as a private business. This was accepted and I was made redundant at the end of August 1992.

However, while negotiations on how the Centre was to be run were in progress, Parliament passed an act which was to make further education colleges independent corporations and enable them to lay claim to the property they used. In November 1992 North Hertfordshire College expressed an interest in the Ashwell site; if they had succeeded they would have taken over the lease from the Merchant Taylors' Company. My attempts to negotiate with them to

Merchant Taylors' School

secure a licence proved fruitless as the College seemed to be uncertain as to whether they really did want to take on the site. In August 1993 they declared that they had no interest in the Centre other than to run adult education classes. In the meantime the then-Warden, Lis Short, had taken voluntary redundancy and I was appointed to run the adult education programme for the College. I now had to start negotiations with the County Council. These were delayed as Hertfordshire County Council were unable to get the information they needed from the College.

The situation now is that the County Council are still the leaseholders of the property and responsible to the Merchant Taylors' Company for the site. I am their Site Manager. The Library not only continues to flourish but has increased its opening hours. North Hertfordshire College uses the premises for adult education classes. I am licensed by Hertfordshire County Council to run my two businesses here - Ashwell Education Services, which runs the Ashwell Field Studies Centre, and Ashwell Business Centre.

It looks therefore as if the future of the Centre is secure. Because of their confidence in the future of the Centre the Governors have recently spent some money on improvements to provide an enclosed porch with a ramp and a separate entrance into the office and kitchen; this will allow the library to be used as a room in its own right and extend its use.

Without the tremendous support from the village it is almost certain that the Centre would have been closed. However, to ensure its future, the activities at the Centre need your continuing support. If you have any ideas for activities please do not hesitate to contact me.

As a school and as a further education centre the Merchant Taylors' School has played an important role in the village since 1681. With your support, it will carry on.